Tower Low Fat Air Fryer Cookbook For Beginners

Easy Recipes for Your Tower T14001

Health Halogen Low Fat Air Fryer

Albert A. Smith

© Copyright 2021 Albert A. Smith - All Rights Reserved.

In no way is it legal to reproduce, duplicate, or transmit any part of this document by either electronic means or in printed format. Recording of this publication is strictly prohibited, and any storage of this material is not allowed unless with written permission from the publisher. All rights reserved.

The information provided herein is stated to be truthful and consistent, in that any liability, regarding inattention or otherwise, by any usage or abuse of any policies, processes, or directions contained within is the solitary and complete responsibility of the recipient reader. Under no circumstances will any legal liability or blame be held against the publisher for any reparation, damages, or monetary loss due to the information herein, either directly or indirectly.

Respective authors own all copyrights not held by the publisher.

Legal Notice:

This book is copyright protected. This is only for personal use. You cannot amend, distribute, sell, use, quote or paraphrase any part of the content within this book without the consent of the author or copyright owner. Legal action will be pursued if this is breached.

Disclaimer Notice:

Please note the information contained within this document is for educational and entertainment purposes only. Every attempt has been made to provide accurate, up-to-date and reliable, complete information. No warranties of any kind are expressed or implied. Readers acknowledge that the author is not engaging in the rendering of legal, financial, medical or professional advice.

By reading this document, the reader agrees that under no circumstances are we responsible for any losses, direct or indirect, which are incurred as a result of the use of information contained within this document, including, but not limited to, errors, omissions, or inaccuracies.

CONTENTS

Introduction **6**
   How Does an Air Fryer Work? 6
   Is Air Fried Food Healthy? 7
   What is the Benefit of an Air Fryer? 7
   Frequently Asked Questions 8

Breakfast & Brunch Recipes **10**
   Vanilla Toast 10
   Toasties 11
   Strip Steak with Japanese Dipping Sauce 12
   Salmon and Spinach Scramble 13
   Chia and Hemp Pudding 14
   Egg & Mushroom Scramble 15
   Asparagus Frittata 16
   Tomatoes Casserole 17
   Paprika Cauliflower Bake 18
   Banana and Hazelnut Muffins 19
   Cheese Pie 20
   Black's Bangin' Casserole 21

Lunch & Dinner Recipes **22**
   Thyme Green Beans 22
   Chicken-mushroom Casserole 23
   Cauliflower Cheese Tater Tots 24
   Lemon Cauliflower and Spinach 25
   Summer Rolls 26
   Meatballs Sandwich Delight 27
   Sriracha Cauliflower 28
   Sprouts and Chicken Casserole 29
   Chicken, Eggs and Lettuce Salad 30
   Chicken Rolls 31
   Portabella Pizza 32

Desserts Recipes **33**
   Chocolate Birthday Cake 33
   Grape Stew 34
   Choco Mug Cake 35
   Old-fashioned Walnut and Rum Cookies 36
   Quick 'n Easy Pumpkin Pie 37
   Mom's Orange Rolls 38
   Pineapple Sticks 39
   Cardamom Bombs 39

Clove Crackers..40
Apple Caramel Relish...41
Strawberry Cheese Cake..42

Beef, pork & Lamb Recipes...43
Bacon Wrapped Pork Tenderloin..43
Herbs Crumbed Rack of Lamb..44
Fried Steak...45
Beef and Thyme Cabbage Mix..46
Festive Teriyaki Beef...47
Beef with Green Parmesan Salad...48
Caramelized Pork..49
Sweet & Sour Pork Chops...50
Cream Cheese Pork...51
Onion'n Garlic Rubbed Trip Tip..52
Beef & Broccoli..53

Fish & Seafood Recipes...54
Oregano Salmon..54
Cajun Shrimp...55
Crumbly Fishcakes..56
Butter Crab Muffins...57
Sesame Seeds Coated Haddock..58
Hot Tilapia...59
Golden Cod Fish Nuggets..60
Pesto Haddock...61
Spanish Salmon Recipe...62
Sesame Tuna Steak...63
Fried Branzino...64

Poultry Recipes..65
Crusted Chicken..65
Five Spice Duck Legs...66
Texas Bbq Chicken Thighs..67
Duck Breasts and Raspberry Sauce Recipe...68
Authentic Mexican Mole...69
Lemon and Chili Chicken Drumsticks..70
Bacon-wrapped Chicken...71
Turkey & Veggie Skewers...72
Garden Vegetable and Chicken Casserole...73
Naked Cheese, Chicken Stuffing 'n Green Beans..74
Middle Eastern Chicken Bbq with Tzatziki Sauce...75

Vegetable & Side Dishes...76
Greek-style Roasted Vegetable Salad...76
Asparagus and Green Beans Salad...77
Roasted Brussels Sprout Salad...78

Parmesan Cauliflower Risotto 79
Gluten-free Beans 80
Coconut Celery and Broccoli Mash 81
Sweet Corn Fritters 82
Fried Yellow Beans with Blue Cheese and Pecans 83
Mushroom Cakes 84
Japanese Tempura Bowl 85
Hot Broccoli 86

Snacks & Appetizers Recipes 87
Feta Triangles 87
Party Chicken Pillows 88
Cheese Filled Bell Peppers 89
Snack Mix 90
Bbq Lil Smokies 91
Broccoli Fries with Spicy Dip 92
Bacon Dip 93
Cheesy Potatoes 94
Broccoli Florets 95
Barbecue Little Smokies 96
Masala Cashew 97

Vegan & Vegetarian Recipes 98
Root Vegetable Medley 98
Crispy Asparagus Dipped in Paprika-garlic Spice 99
Roasted Mushrooms in Herb-garlic Oil 100
Aromatic Baked Potatoes with Chives 101
Thai Sweet Potato Balls 102
Broccoli with Olives 103
Cheddar, Squash 'n Zucchini Casserole 104
Spiced Up Potato Wedges 105
Grilled 'n Glazed Strawberries 106
Teriyaki Cauliflower4 107
Paneer Cutlet 108

INTRODUCTION

What is an Air Fryer?

What is an air fryer? This is a question many consumers are still asking. The name can be misleading, as this air cooker does much more than fry up diet-busting treats. It roasts, grills, fries, and even BAKES!

We're here to demystify the inner workings and results of this handy kitchen appliance.

Below, you'll learn how the air fryer uses convection currents to cook your foods, examine comparisons to similar kitchen products, discover amazing uses for this device, and more.

How Does an Air Fryer Work?

Air fryers simulate the traditional frying of foods by circulating hot air around food rather than submerging the food in oil. As with frying, properly prepared foods are crispy, juicy, golden brown, and flavorful.

Air fryers work due to the Maillard reaction, a scientific principle which refers to what we usually call "browning." A Maillard reaction occurs when the surface of a food item forms a crust due to dehydration, and the intense heat breaks down proteins, starches, and fibers. That is what gives fried, roasted, and baked foods their delicious, complex flavors.

An air fryer is a convection oven in miniature – a compact cylindrical countertop convection oven, to be exact (try saying that three times fast).

Basically, convection is the tendency of gases (or liquids) to move past each other when heated. Hot air rises, for example, simultaneously forcing cooler air to sink. Convection influences the weather; it is even at work in the molten rock that causes volcanic eruptions. But what, you may ask, does this have to do with your kitchen appliances?

Air fryers employ convection to rapidly and efficiently cook crisp foods. A heating element within the air fryer super-heats the air, producing natural convection currents. A fan within the appliance aids in air movement, circulating it even more rapidly. Perforations or holes in the cooking basket allow the hot air to flow freely around the food. This air movement increases heat transfer from the air to the food. Thus, your dinner gets done faster.

Is Air Fried Food Healthy?

Does an Air Fryer Use Radiation?

No. Unlike microwave ovens, which use a form of electromagnetic radiation called microwaves to excite water molecules, thus heating the food due to friction, air fryers do not use any form of radiation. Instead, air fryers employ a heating element similar to that found on any oven, toaster, or stovetop. The heating element works by converting an electrical current into heat.

Do Air Fryers Really Work?

We've already discussed how air fryers work. Now, you want to know, do they work, that is, do they work as shown on television commercials? Can they prepare crispy, amazing foods as advertised? Are air fryers worth the hype?

When used as designed and with quality recipes, air fryers do work. You can make crispy French fries, juicy roasted poultry, air fried veggies, and more. You may wish to consult our air fryer cooking charts to learn the best temperature at which to cook your favorite foods, and for how long.

What is the Benefit of an Air Fryer?

Consider the following reasons why an air fryer might be right for you:

Healthy Cooking

Everyone loves the taste of deep-fried foods, but many people must avoid these for health reasons. If you're looking to lower cholesterol or lose weight, your doctor may thank you for using an air fryer. Air fryers use around 75 percent less oil than deep fryers, providing a healthy alternative without sacrificing flavor.

Speed of Cooking

The air fryer's small convection oven preheats and cooks more quickly than a conventional oven. You'll have tasty meals in haste, with less wait!

Green Cooking

Have you "gone green?" Cooking with an air fryer can help. Most air fryers are energy efficient, and shorter cook times translate to less overall power usage.

Simple and Easy

Air fryers utilize simple controls, typically two knobs for cook time and temperature, or an easy to read digital display. You simply toss the food in oil (if desired), place it in the basket, and the air fryer does the rest.

Clean Up Is a Breeze

The baskets and pans of most air fryers are dishwasher safe for easy cleanup. Also, the enclosed nature of the air fryer prevents the splatters and spills associated with deep frying and pan frying.

Safe

Lacking the large oil vats of traditional deep fryers, air fryers eliminate the risk of serious burns from spilled oil. Also, air fryers are designed so that the exterior does not become dangerously hot to the touch.

Frequently Asked Questions

What Types of Oils Can I Use in An Air Fryer?

Your oil mister will work great with any oils that have a high smoke point. This means the oil will withstand high temperatures before burning.

Avocado oil has a high smoke point of 570 degrees and gives food exceptional flavor. Other good choices include light olive oil (468 degrees), refined coconut oil (450 degrees), and peanut oil (450 degrees). You'll find that Bertolli brand oil and grapeseed oils are reliable.

Do You Put Oil in an Air Fryer?

An air fryer can prepare foods that would normally go in a deep fryer. Spraying foods like fries or onion rings with oil allows the intense circulating heat of the machine to cook a crisp exterior and tender interior. Most recipes only call for about 1 tbsp. of oil, which is best applied with a mister.

Fatty foods, like bacon, won't need you to add any oil. Leaner meats, however, will need some oiling to keep them from sticking to the pan.

Is Airfryer better than oven?

Do Air Fryers Work Better Than an Oven?

While air fryers and convection ovens both employ the science of convection, they have distinct differences in function and design. Both appliances may reduce cooking times due to fan-circulated, heated air.

Countertop convection ovens are generally larger than air fryers. They are designed for larger batch cooking, while air fryers typically handle two to six servings at a time.

Air fryers are easier to clean due to dishwasher safe parts and are very versatile when used with accessories.

What Can You Cook with an Air Fryer?

French fries, tater tots, onion rings, and homemade potato chips

Baked potatoes

Grilled cheese sandwiches

Roasted vegetables

Corn on the cob

Single-serve pizza

Empanadas

Egg rolls, spring rolls, and crab rangoon

Donut holes

Chicken

Hamburgers

Bacon

Fish

Steak

Steak? Yes, you read that right. You can cook juicy, tender steaks in an air fryer. Pizza? Well, a whole frozen pizza won't fit, but you can reheat leftovers like a champ, or make your own small, single serving pizzas using pita or naan bread.

As you can see, the possibilities are almost endless. If you can cook it at home, you'll most likely be able to cook it in your air fryer.

BREAKFAST & BRUNCH RECIPES

Vanilla Toast

Servings: 6
Cooking Time: 10 Mins.

Ingredients:
- ½ cup sugar
- 1 ½ tsp cinnamon
- 1 stick of butter, softened
- 1 tsp vanilla extract

Directions:
1. Preheat the air fryer to 400 F. Combine all ingredients, except the bread, in a bowl. Spread the buttery cinnamon mixture onto the bread slices. Place the bread slices in the air fryer. Cook for 5 minutes.

Toasties

Servings: 2
Cooking Time: 30 Mins.

Ingredients:
- ¼ cup milk or cream
- 2 sausages, boiled
- 3 eggs
- 1 slice bread, sliced lengthwise
- 4 tbsp. cheese, grated
- Sea salt to taste
- Chopped fresh herbs and steamed broccoli [optional]

Directions:
1. Pre-heat your Air Fryer at 360°F and set the timer for 5 minutes.
2. In the meantime, scramble the eggs in a bowl and add in the milk.
3. Grease three muffin cups with a cooking spray. Divide the egg mixture in three and pour equal amounts into each cup.
4. Slice the sausages and drop them, along with the slices of bread, into the egg mixture. Add the cheese on top and a little salt as desired.
5. Transfer the cups to the Fryer and cook for 15-20 minutes, depending on how firm you would like them. When ready, remove them from the fryer and serve with fresh herbs and steam broccoli if you prefer.

Strip Steak with Japanese Dipping Sauce

Servings: 2
Cooking Time: 40 Mins.

Ingredients:
- 2 strip steaks
- Salt and pepper to taste
- 1 tbsp. olive oil
- ½ cup soy sauce
- ½ cup rice wine vinegar
- ¼ cup grated daikon radish

Directions:
1. Preheat the air fryer at 390F.
2. Place the grill pan accessory in the air fryer.
3. Season the steak with salt and pepper.
4. Brush with oil.
5. Grill for 20 minutes per piece and make sure to flip the beef halfway through the cooking time
6. Prepare the dipping sauce by combining the soy sauce and vinegar.
7. Serve the steak with the sauce and daikon radish.

Salmon and Spinach Scramble

Servings: 4
Cooking Time: 20 Mins.

Ingredients:
- A drizzle of olive oil
- 1 spring onion, chopped
- 1 cup smoked salmon, skinless, boneless and flaked
- 4 eggs, whisked
- A pinch of salt and black pepper
- ¼ cup baby spinach
- 4 tbsp. parmesan, grated

Directions:
1. In a bowl, mix the eggs with the rest of the ingredients except the oil and whisk well. Grease the Air Fryer with the oil, preheat it at 360 degrees F, pour the eggs and salmon mix and cook for 20 minutes. Divide between plates and serve for breakfast.

Chia and Hemp Pudding

Servings: 2
Cooking Time: 2 Mins.

Ingredients:
- 1 tsp. hemp seeds
- 1 tsp. chia seeds
- 1 tbsp. almond flour
- 1 tsp. coconut flakes
- 1 tsp. walnuts, chopped
- ½ tsp. flax meal
- ¼ tsp. vanilla extract
- ½ tsp. Erythritol
- ½ cup of coconut milk
- ¼ cup water, boiled

Directions:
1. Put hemp seeds, chia seeds, almond flour, coconut flakes, walnuts, flax meal, vanilla extract, coconut milk, and water in the big bowl. Stir the mixture until homogenous and pour it into 2 mason jars. Leave the mason jars in the cold place for 4 hours. Then top the surface of the pudding with Erythritol. Place the mason jars in the air fryer and cook the pudding for 2 minutes at 400F or until you get the light brown crust.

Egg & Mushroom Scramble

Servings: 2
Cooking Time: 10 Mins.

Ingredients:
- 4 eggs
- Salt and freshly ground black pepper, as needed
- 2 tbsps. unsalted butter
- ½ cup fresh mushrooms, finely chopped
- 2 tbsps. Parmesan cheese, shredded

Directions:
1. Set the temperature of Air Fryer to 285 degrees F.
2. In a bowl, mix together the eggs, salt, and black pepper.
3. In a baking pan, melt the butter and tilt the pan to spread the butter in the bottom.
4. Add the beaten eggs and Air Fry for about 4-5 Mins.
5. Add in the mushrooms and cheese and cook for 5 minutes, stirring occasionally.
6. Serve hot.

Asparagus Frittata

Servings: 4
Cooking Time: 10 Mins.

Ingredients:
- 6 eggs
- 3 mushrooms, sliced
- 10 asparagus, chopped
- 1/4 cup half and half
- 2 tsp butter, melted
- 1 cup mozzarella cheese, shredded
- 1 tsp pepper
- 1 tsp salt

Directions:
1. Toss mushrooms and asparagus with melted butter and add into the air fryer basket.
2. Cook mushrooms and asparagus at 350 F for 5 minutes. Shake basket twice.
3. Meanwhile, in a bowl, whisk together eggs, half and half, pepper, and salt.
4. Transfer cook mushrooms and asparagus into the air fryer baking dish.
5. Pour egg mixture over mushrooms and asparagus.
6. Place dish in the air fryer and cook at 350 F for 5 minutes or until eggs are set.
7. Slice and serve.

Tomatoes Casserole

Servings: 4
Cooking Time: 15 Mins.

Ingredients:
- 4 eggs, whisked
- 1 tsp. olive oil
- 3 ozs. Swiss chard, chopped
- 1 cup tomatoes, cubed
- Salt and black pepper to the taste

Directions:
1. In a bowl, mix the eggs with the rest of the ingredients except the oil and whisk well. Grease a pan that fits the fryer with the oil, pour the swish chard mix and cook at 359 degrees F for 15 minutes. Divide between plates and serve for breakfast.

Paprika Cauliflower Bake

Servings: 4
Cooking Time: 20 Mins.

Ingredients:
- 2 cups cauliflower florets, separated
- 4 eggs, whisked
- 1 tsp. sweet paprika
- 2 tbsps. butter, melted
- A pinch of salt and black pepper

Directions:
1. Heat up your air fryer at 320 degrees F, grease with the butter, add cauliflower florets on the bottom, then add eggs whisked with paprika, salt and pepper, toss and cook for 20 minutes. Divide between plates and serve for breakfast.

Banana and Hazelnut Muffins

Servings: 6
Cooking Time: 40 Mins.

Ingredients:
- ½ cup honey
- 2 eggs, lightly beaten
- 4 ripe bananas, mashed
- 1 tsp vanilla extract
- 2 cups flour
- 1 tsp baking powder
- ½ tsp baking soda
- 1 tsp ground cinnamon
- ½ cup chopped hazelnuts
- ½ cup dark chocolate chips

Directions:
1. Spray 10-hole muffin with oil spray. in a bowl, whisk butter, honey, eggs, bananas, and vanilla, until well-combine. Sift in flour, baking powder, baking soda, and cinnamon without overmixing.
2. Stir in the hazelnuts and chocolate into the mixture. Pour the mixture into the muffin holes and place in the air fryer. Cook for 30 minutes at 350 F, checking them at the around 20-minute mark.

Cheese Pie

Servings: 4
Cooking Time: 16 Mins.

Ingredients:
- 8 eggs
- 1 1/2 cups heavy whipping cream
- 1 lb cheddar cheese, grated
- Pepper
- Salt

Directions:
1. Preheat the air fryer to 325 F.
2. In a bowl, whisk together cheese, eggs, whipping cream, pepper, and salt.
3. Spray air fryer baking dish with cooking spray.
4. Pour egg mixture into the prepared dish and place in the air fryer basket.
5. Cook for 16 minutes or until the egg is set.
6. Serve and enjoy.

Black's Bangin' Casserole

Servings: 4
Cooking Time: 40 Mins.

Ingredients:

- 5 eggs
- 3 tbsp chunky tomato sauce
- 2 tbsp heavy cream
- 2 tbsp grated parmesan cheese

Directions:

1. Preheat your fryer to 350°F/175°C.
2. Combine the eggs and cream in a bowl.
3. Mix in the tomato sauce and add the cheese.
4. Spread into a glass baking dish and bake for 25-35 minutes.
5. Top with extra cheese.
6. Enjoy!

LUNCH & DINNER RECIPES

Thyme Green Beans

Servings: 6
Cooking Time: 20 Mins.

Ingredients:
- 1 lb. green beans, trimmed and halved
- 2 eggplants, cubed
- 1 cup veggie stock
- 1 tbsp. olive oil
- 1 red chili pepper
- 1 red bell pepper, chopped
- ½ tsp. thyme, dried
- Salt and black pepper to the taste

Directions:
1. In a pan that fits your air fryer, mix all the ingredients, toss, introduce the pan in the machine and cook at 350 degrees F for 20 minutes. Divide into bowls and serve for lunch.

Chicken-mushroom Casserole

Servings: 4
Cooking Time: 30 Mins.

Ingredients:
- 4 chicken breasts
- ½ cup shredded cheese
- Salt to taste
- 1 cup coconut milk
- 1 cup mushrooms
- 1 broccoli, cut into florets
- 1 tbsp. curry powder

Directions:
1. Pre-heat your Air Fryer to 350°F. Spritz a casserole dish with some cooking spray.
2. Cube the chicken breasts and combine with curry powder and coconut milk in a bowl. Season with salt.
3. Add in the broccoli and mushroom and mix well.
4. Pour the mixture into the casserole dish. Top with the cheese.
5. Transfer to your Air Fryer and cook for about 20 minutes.
6. Serve warm.

Cauliflower Cheese Tater Tots

Servings: 12
Cooking Time: 25 Mins.

Ingredients:
- 1 lb. cauliflower, steamed and chopped
- ½ cup nutritional yeast
- 1 tbsp. oats
- 1 flax egg [1 tbsp. desiccated coconuts + 3 tbsp. flaxseed meal
- + 3 tbsp. water]
- 1 onion, chopped
- 1 tsp. garlic, minced
- 1 tsp. parsley, chopped
- 1 tsp. oregano, chopped
- 1 tsp. chives, chopped
- Salt and pepper to taste
- ½ cup bread crumbs

Directions:
1. Pre-heat the Air Fryer at 390°F.
2. Drain any excess water out of the cauliflower by wringing it with a paper towel.
3. In a bowl, combine the cauliflower with the remaining ingredients, save the bread crumbs. Using your hands, shape the mixture into several small balls.
4. Coat the balls in the bread crumbs and transfer to the basket of your fryer. Allow to cook for 6 minutes, after which you should raise the temperature to 400°F and then leave to cook for an additional 10 minutes.

Lemon Cauliflower and Spinach

Servings: 4
Cooking Time: 20 Mins.

Ingredients:
- 1-pound cauliflower head
- 1 tbsp. olive oil
- 1 tsp. lemon juice
- 1 tsp. salt
- 1 tsp. chili flakes
- 2 cups of water
- 6 bacon slices
- ½ cup spinach, chopped
- ½ cup Cheddar cheese, shredded
- ½ tsp. minced garlic
- 1 egg, beaten
- 1 tbsp. mascarpone

Directions:
1. Pour water in the saucepan and bring it to boil. Then add olive oil, lemon juice, salt, and chili flakes. Put the cauliflower head in the boiling water and simmer it for 10 minutes with the closed lid. Meanwhile, mix up minced ginger, egg, mascarpone, Cheddar cheese, and spinach. You should get a smooth and homogenous mixture. After this, cool the cooked cauliflower head and fill it with the spinach mixture. After this, wrap the cauliflower head in the bacon. Preheat the air fryer to 400F. Place the wrapped cauliflower head in the air fryer basket and cook it for 10 minutes or until bacon is light brown. Cut the cooked cauliflower head on 4 servings.

Summer Rolls

Servings: 4
Cooking Time: 25 Mins.

Ingredients:
- 1 cup shiitake mushroom, sliced thinly
- 1 celery stalk, chopped
- 1 medium carrot, shredded
- ½ tsp. ginger, finely chopped
- 1 tsp. sugar
- 1 tbsp. soy sauce
- 1 tsp. nutritional yeast
- 8 spring roll sheets
- 1 tsp. corn starch
- 2 tbsp. water

Directions:
1. In a bowl, combine the ginger, soy sauce, nutritional yeast, carrots, celery, and sugar.
2. Mix together the cornstarch and water to create an adhesive for your spring rolls.
3. Scoop a tablespoonful of the vegetable mixture into the middle of the spring roll sheets. Brush the edges of the sheets with the cornstarch adhesive and enclose around the filling to make spring rolls.
4. Pre-heat your Air Fryer at 400°F. When warm, place the rolls inside and cook for 15 minutes or until crisp.

Meatballs Sandwich Delight

Servings: 4
Cooking Time: 32 Mins.

Ingredients:
- 3 baguettes; sliced more than halfway through
- 14 oz. beef; ground
- 1 tbsp. olive oil
- 1 tsp. thyme; dried
- 1 tsp. basil; dried
- 7 oz. tomato sauce
- 1 small onion; chopped
- 1 egg; whisked
- 1 tbsp. bread crumbs
- 2 tbsp. cheddar cheese; grated
- 1 tbsp. oregano; chopped
- Salt and black pepper to the taste

Directions:
1. In a bowl; combine meat with salt, pepper, onion, breadcrumbs, egg, cheese, oregano, thyme and basil; stir, shape medium meatballs and add them to your air fryer after you've greased it with the oil.
2. Cook them at 375 °F, for 12 minutes; flipping them halfway.
3. Add tomato sauce, cook meatballs for 10 minutes more and arrange them on sliced baguettes. Serve them right away.

Sriracha Cauliflower

Servings: 4
Cooking Time: 25 Mins.

Ingredients:
- ¼ cup vegan butter, melted
- ¼ cup sriracha sauce
- 4 cups cauliflower florets
- 1 cup bread crumbs
- 1 tsp. salt

Directions:
1. Mix together the sriracha and vegan butter in a bowl and pour this mixture over the cauliflower, taking care to cover each floret entirely.
2. In a separate bowl, combine the bread crumbs and salt.
3. Dip the cauliflower florets in the bread crumbs, coating each one well. Cook in the Air Fryer for 17 minutes in a 375°F pre-heated Air Fryer.

Sprouts and Chicken Casserole

Servings: 2
Cooking Time: 25 Mins.

Ingredients:
- 1 cup Brussels sprouts
- ½ tsp. salt
- ½ cup ground chicken
- ½ tsp. ground black pepper
- 1 tbsp. coconut cream
- 1 tsp. chili powder
- 1 tbsp. butter, melted
- ½ tsp. ground paprika

Directions:
1. Mix up ground chicken, ground black pepper, chili powder, ground paprika, and coconut cream. Add salt and stir the mixture. After this, grease the air fryer casserole mold with butter. Put Brussels sprouts in the casserole mold and flatten them in one layer. Then top the vegetables with ground chicken mixture. Cover the casserole with baking paper and secure the edges. Preheat the air fryer to 365F. Put the casserole mold in the air fryer basket and cook it for 25 minutes.

Chicken, Eggs and Lettuce Salad

Servings: 3
Cooking Time: 8 Mins.

Ingredients:
- 3 spring onions, sliced
- 8 oz chicken fillet, roughly chopped
- 1 bacon slice, cooked, crumbled
- 2 cherry tomatoes, halved
- ¼ avocado, chopped
- 2 eggs, hard-boiled, peeled, chopped
- 1 cup lettuce, roughly chopped
- 1 tbsp. sesame oil
- ½ tsp. lemon juice
- ½ tsp. avocado oil
- ½ tsp. ground black pepper
- ½ tsp. salt
- 1 egg, beaten
- 2 tbsps. coconut flakes

Directions:
1. Sprinkle the chopped chicken fillets with salt and ground black pepper. Then dip the chicken in the egg and after this, coat in the coconut flakes. Preheat the air fryer to 385F. Place the chicken fillets inside and sprinkle them with avocado oil. Cook the chicken pieces for 8 minutes. Shake them after 4 minutes of cooking. After this, in the mixing bowl mix up spring onions, bacon, cherry tomatoes, hard-boiled eggs, lettuce, and lemon juice. Add sesame oil and shake the salad well. When the chicken is cooked, add it in the cobb salad and mix up gently with the help of the wooden spatulas.

Chicken Rolls

Servings: 4
Cooking Time: 18 Mins.

Ingredients:
- 2 large zucchini
- ½ cup Cheddar cheese, shredded
- 1-pound chicken breast, skinless, boneless
- 1 tsp. dried oregano
- ½ tsp. olive oil
- 1 tsp. salt
- 2 spring onions, chopped
- 1 tsp. ground paprika
- ½ tsp. ground turmeric
- ½ cup keto tomato sauce

Directions:
1. Preheat the skillet well and pour the olive oil inside. Put the onions in it and sprinkle with salt, ground paprika, and ground turmeric. Cook the onion for 5 minutes over the medium-high heat. Stir it from time to time. Meanwhile, shred the chicken. Add it in the skillet. Then add oregano. Stir well and cook the mixture for 2 minutes. After this, remove the skillet from the heat. Cut the zucchini into halves (lengthwise). Then make the zucchini slices with the help of the vegetable peeler. Put 3 zucchini slices on the chopping board overlapping each of them. Then spread the surface of them with the shredded chicken mixture. Roll the zucchini carefully in the shape of the roll. Repeat the same steps with remaining zucchini and shredded chicken mixture. Line the air fryer pan with parchment and put the enchilada rolls inside. Sprinkle them with tomato sauce Preheat the air fryer to 350F. Top the zucchini rolls (enchiladas) with Cheddar cheese and put in the air fryer basket. Cook the meal for 10 minutes.

Portabella Pizza

Servings: 3
Cooking Time: 15 Mins.

Ingredients:
- 3 tbsp. olive oil
- 3 portobello mushroom caps, cleaned and scooped
- 3 tbsp. mozzarella, shredded
- 3 tbsp. tomato sauce
- Pinch of salt
- 12 slices pepperoni
- Pinch of dried Italian seasonings

Directions:
1. Pre-heat the Air Fryer to 330°F.
2. Coat both sides of the mushroom cap with a drizzle of oil, before seasoning the inside with the Italian seasonings and salt. Evenly spread the tomato sauce over the mushroom and add the cheese on top.
3. Put the mushroom into the cooking basket of the Air Fryer. Place the slices of pepperoni on top of the portobello pizza after a minute of cooking and continue to cook for another 3-5 minutes.

DESSERTS RECIPES

Chocolate Birthday Cake

Servings: 6
Cooking Time: 35 Minutes + Chilling Time

Ingredients:
- 2 eggs, beaten
- 2/3 cup sour cream
- 1 cup flour
- 1/2 cup sugar
- 1/4 cup honey
- 1/3 cup coconut oil, softened
- 1/4 cup cocoa powder
- 2 tbsps. chocolate chips
- 1 ½ tsps. baking powder
- 1 tsp. vanilla extract
- 1/2 tsp. pure rum extract
- Chocolate Frosting:
- 1/2 cup butter, softened
- 1/4 cup cocoa powder
- 2 cups powdered sugar
- 2 tbsps. milk

Directions:
1. Mix all ingredients for the chocolate cake with a hand mixer on low speed. Scrape the batter into a cake pan.
2. Bake at 330 degrees F for 25 to 30 minutes. Transfer the cake to a wire rack
3. Meanwhile, whip the butter and cocoa until smooth. Stir in the powdered sugar. Slowly and gradually, pour in the milk until your frosting reaches desired consistency.
4. Whip until smooth and fluffy; then, frost the cooled cake. Place in your refrigerator for a couple of hours. Serve well chilled.

Grape Stew

Servings: 4
Cooking Time: 14 Mins.

Ingredients:
- 1 lb. red grapes
- Juice and zest of 1 lemon
- 26 ozs. grape juice

Directions:
1. In a pan that fits your air fryer, add all ingredients and toss.
2. Place the pan in the fryer and cook at 320 degrees F for 14 minutes.
3. Divide into cups, refrigerate, and serve cold.

Choco Mug Cake

Servings: 1
Cooking Time: 20 Mins.

Ingredients:
- 1 egg, lightly beaten
- 1 tbsp heavy cream
- ¼ tsp baking powder
- 2 tbsp unsweetened cocoa powder
- 2 tbsp Erythritol
- ½ tsp vanilla
- 1 tbsp peanut butter
- 1 tsp salt

Directions:
1. Preheat the air fryer to 400 F.
2. In a bowl, mix together all ingredients until well combined.
3. Spray mug with cooking spray.
4. Pour batter in mug and place in the air fryer and cook for 20 minutes.
5. Serve and enjoy.

Old-fashioned Walnut and Rum Cookies

Servings: 8
Cooking Time: 40 Mins.

Ingredients:
- 1/2 cup walnuts, ground
- 1/2 cup coconut flour
- 1 cup almond flour
- 3/4 cup swerve
- 1 stick butter, room temperature
- 2 tbsps. rum
- 1/2 tsp. pure vanilla extract
- 1/2 tsp. pure almond extract

Directions:
1. In a mixing dish, beat the butter with swerve, vanilla, and almond extract until light and fluffy. Then, throw in the flour and ground walnuts; add in rum.
2. Continue mixing until it forms a soft dough. Cover and place in the refrigerator for 20 minutes. in the meantime, preheat the Air Fryer to 330 degrees F.
3. Roll the dough into small cookies and place them on the Air Fryer cake pan; gently press each cookie using a spoon.
4. Bake butter cookies for 15 minutes in the preheated Air Fryer. Bon appétit!

Quick 'n Easy Pumpkin Pie

Servings: 8
Cooking Time: 35 Mins.

Ingredients:
- 1 (14 ounce) can sweetened condensed milk
- 1 (15 ounce) can pumpkin puree
- 1 9-inch unbaked pie crust
- 1 large egg
- 1 tsp. ground cinnamon
- 1/2 tsp. fine salt
- 1/2 tsp. ground ginger
- 1/4 tsp. freshly grated nutmeg
- 1/8 tsp. Chinese 5-spice powder
- 3 egg yolks

Directions:
1. Lightly grease baking pan of air fryer with cooking spray. Press pie crust on bottom of pan, stretching all the way up to the sides of the pan. Pierce all over with fork.
2. In blender, blend well egg, egg yolks, and pumpkin puree. Add Chinese 5-spice powder, nutmeg, salt, ginger, cinnamon, and condensed milk. Pour on top of pie crust.
3. Cover pan with foil.
4. For 15 minutes, cook on preheated 390oF air fryer.
5. Remove foil and continue cooking for 20 minutes at 330oF until middle is set.
6. Allow to cool in air fryer completely.
7. Serve and enjoy.

Mom's Orange Rolls

Servings: 6
Cooking Time: 1 Hour 20 Mins.

Ingredients:
- 1/2 cup milk
- 1/4 cup granulated sugar
- 1 tbsp. yeast
- 1/2 stick butter, at room temperature
- 1 egg, at room temperature
- 1/4 tsp. salt
- 2 cups all-purpose flour
- 2 tbsps. fresh orange juice
- Filling:
- 2 tbsps. butter
- 4 tbsps. white sugar
- 1 tsp. ground star anise
- 1/4 tsp. ground cinnamon
- 1 tsp. vanilla paste
- 1/2 cup confectioners' sugar

Directions:
1. Heat the milk in a microwave safe bowl and transfer the warm milk to the bowl of a stand electric mixer. Add the granulated sugar and yeast, and mix to combine well. Cover and let it sit until the yeast is foamy.
2. Then, beat the butter on low speed. Fold in the egg and mix again. Add salt and flour. Add the orange juice and mix on medium speed until a soft dough forms.
3. Knead the dough on a lightly floured surface. Cover it loosely and let it sit in a warm place about 1 hour or until doubled in size. Then, spritz the bottom and sides of a baking pan with cooking oil (butter flavored.
4. Roll your dough out into a rectangle.
5. Spread 2 tbsps. of butter all over the dough. in a mixing dish, combine the white sugar, ground star anise, cinnamon, and vanilla; sprinkle evenly over the dough.
6. Then, roll up your dough to form a log. Cut into 6 equal rolls and place them in the parchment-lined Air Fryer basket.
7. Bake at 350 degrees for 12 minutes, turning them halfway through the cooking time. Dust with confectioners' sugar and enjoy!

Pineapple Sticks

Servings: 4
Cooking Time: 20 Mins.

Ingredients:
- ½ fresh pineapple, cut into sticks
- ¼ cup desiccated coconut

Directions:
1. Pre-heat the Air Fryer to 400°F.
2. Coat the pineapple sticks in the desiccated coconut and put each one in the Air Fryer basket.
3. Air fry for 10 minutes.

Cardamom Bombs

Servings: 2
Cooking Time: 5 Mins.

Ingredients:
- 2 oz avocado, peeled
- 1 egg, beaten
- ½ tsp. ground cardamom
- 1 tbsp. Erythritol
- 2 tbsps. coconut flour
- 1 tsp. butter, softened

Directions:
1. Put the avocado in the bowl and mash it with the help of the fork. Add egg and stir the mixture until it is smooth. Then add ground cardamom, Erythritol, and coconut flour. After this, add butter and stir the mixture well. Make the balls from the avocado mixture and press them gently. Then preheat the air fryer to 400F. Put the avocado bombs in the air fryer and cook them for 5 minutes.

Clove Crackers

Servings: 8
Cooking Time: 33 Mins.

Ingredients:
- 1 cup almond flour
- 1 tsp. xanthan gum
- 1 tsp. flax meal
- ½ tsp. salt
- 1 tsp. baking powder
- 1 tsp. lemon juice
- ½ tsp. ground clove
- 2 tbsps. Erythritol
- 1 egg, beaten
- 3 tbsps. coconut oil, softened

Directions:
1. In the mixing bowl mix up almond flour, xanthan gum, flax meal, salt, baking powder, and ground clove. Add Erythritol, lemon juice, egg, and coconut oil. Stir the mixture gently with the help of the fork. Then knead the mixture till you get a soft dough. Line the chopping board with parchment. Put the dough on the parchment and roll it up in a thin layer. Cut the thin dough into squares (crackers). Preheat the air fryer to 360F. Line the air fryer basket with baking paper. Put the prepared crackers in the air fryer basket in one layer and cook them for 11 minutes or until the crackers are dry and light brown. Repeat the same steps with remaining uncooked crackers.

Apple Caramel Relish

Servings: 4
Cooking Time: 40 Mins.

Ingredients:
- 2 apples, peeled, sliced
- 3 oz butter, melted
- ½ cup brown sugar
- 1 tsp cinnamon
- ½ cup flour
- 1 cup caramel sauce

Directions:
1. Line a cake tin with baking paper. in a bowl, mix butter, sugar, cinnamon and flour until you obtain a crumbly texture. Prepare the cake mix according to the instructions (no baking). Pour the batter into the tin and arrange the apple slices on top. Spoon the caramel over the apples and add the crumble over the sauce. Cook in the air fryer for 35 minutes at 360 F; make sure to check it halfway through, so it's not overcooked.

Strawberry Cheese Cake

Servings: 6
Cooking Time: 35 Mins.

Ingredients:
- 1 cup almond flour
- 3 tbsp coconut oil, melted
- ½ tsp vanilla
- 1 egg, lightly beaten
- 1 tbsp fresh lime juice
- ¼ cup erythritol
- 1 cup cream cheese, softened
- 1 lb strawberries, chopped
- 2 tsp baking powder

Directions:
1. Add all ingredients into the large bowl and mix until well combined.
2. Spray air fryer cake pan with cooking spray.
3. Pour batter into the prepared pan and place into the air fryer and cook at 350 F for 35 minutes.
4. Allow to cool completely.
5. Slice and serve.

BEEF, PORK & LAMB RECIPES

Bacon Wrapped Pork Tenderloin

Servings: 4
Cooking Time: 30 Mins.

Ingredients:
- 1 (1½ pound) pork tenderloins
- 4 bacon strips
- 2 tbsps. Dijon mustard

Directions:
1. Preheat the Air fryer to 360 o F and grease an Air fryer basket.
2. Rub the tenderloin evenly with mustard and wrap the tenderloin with bacon strips.
3. Arrange the pork tenderloin in the Air fryer basket and cook for about 30 minutes, flipping once in between.
4. Dish out the steaks and cut into desired size slices to serve.

Herbs Crumbed Rack of Lamb

Servings: 5
Cooking Time: 30 Mins.

Ingredients:
- 1 tbsp. butter, melted
- 1 garlic clove, finely chopped
- 1¾ lbs. rack of lamb
- Salt and ground black pepper, as required
- 1 egg
- ½ cup panko breadcrumbs
- 1 tbsp. fresh thyme, minced
- 1 tbsp. fresh rosemary, minced

Directions:
1. In a bowl, mix together the butter, garlic, salt, and black pepper.
2. Coat the rack of lamb evenly with garlic mixture.
3. In a shallow dish, beat the egg.
4. In another dish, mix together the breadcrumbs and herbs.
5. Dip the rack of lamb in beaten egg and then, coat with breadcrumbs mixture.
6. Set the temperature of air fryer to 212 degrees F. Grease an air fryer basket.
7. Place rack of lamb into the prepared air fryer basket.
8. Air Fry for about 25 minutes and then 5 more minutes at 390 degrees F.
9. Remove from air fryer and place the rack of lamb onto a cutting board for about 5 Mins.
10. With a sharp knife, cut the rack of lamb into individual chops and serve.

Fried Steak

Servings: 1
Cooking Time: 15 Mins.

Ingredients:
- 3 cm-thick beef steak
- Pepper and salt to taste

Directions:
1. Pre-heat the Air Fryer 400°F for 5 minutes.
2. Place the beef steak in the baking tray and sprinkle on pepper and salt.
3. Spritz the steak with cooking spray.
4. Allow to cook for 3 minutes. Turn the steak over and cook on the other side for 3 more minutes. Serve hot.

Beef and Thyme Cabbage Mix

Servings: 4
Cooking Time: 25 Mins.

Ingredients:
- 2 lbs. beef, cubed
- ½ lb. bacon, chopped
- 2 shallots, chopped
- 1 napa cabbage, shredded
- 2 garlic cloves, minced
- A pinch of salt and black pepper
- 2 tbsps. olive oil
- 1 tsp. thyme, dried
- 1 cup beef stock

Directions:
1. Heat up a pan that fits the air fryer with the oil over medium-high heat, add the beef and brown for 3 minutes. Add the bacon, shallots and garlic and cook for 2 minutes more. Add the rest of the ingredients, toss, put the pan in the air fryer and cook at 390 degrees F for 20 minutes. Divide between plates and serve.

Festive Teriyaki Beef

Servings: 4
Cooking Time: 40 Mins.

Ingredients:
- 2 heaping tbsps. fresh parsley, roughly chopped
- 1 lb. beef rump steaks
- 2 heaping tbsps. fresh chives, roughly chopped
- Salt and black pepper (or mixed peppercorns, to savor
- For the Sauce:
- ½ cup grapefruit juice
- 1/3 cup hoisin sauce
- 1 tbsp. fresh ginger, grated
- 1 ½ tbsps. mirin
- 3 garlic cloves, minced
- 2 tbsp. rice bran oil
- ½ cup soy sauce
- 1/3 cup brown sugar

Directions:
1. Firstly, steam the beef rump steaks for 8 minutes (use the method of steaming that you prefer. Season the beef with salt and black pepper; scatter the chopped parsley and chives over the top.
2. Roast the beef rump steaks in an air fryer basket for 28 minutes at 345 degrees, turning halfway through.
3. While the beef is cooking, combine the ingredients for the teriyaki sauce in a sauté pan. Then, let it simmer over low heat until it has thickened.
4. Toss the beef with the teriyaki sauce until it is well covered and serve.

Beef with Green Parmesan Salad

Servings: 2
Cooking Time: 15 Mins.

Ingredients:
- 1/2 cup vegetable stock
- 1/3 cup scallions, chopped
- 1 cloves garlic, minced
- 2 beef chops
- ½ tbsp. melted butter
- Table salt and ground black pepper, to savor
- For the Salad:
- 1 ½ tbsps. freshly grated Parmesan
- 1 tbsp. apple cider vinegar
- 2 tbsps. extra-virgin olive oil
- 2 cups very finely chopped or slivered curly kale
- 1/3 tsp. ground black pepper, or more to taste
- 1 tsp. table salt

Directions:
1. Take an oven safe dish and toss beef chops with salt, pepper, butter, scallions, and garlic; pour in the stock; gently stir to coat.
2. Now, roast your chops at 395 degrees F for 12 to 14 minutes.
3. Meanwhile, make the parmesan-kale salad by mixing all salad components. Serve warm beef chops with the prepared kale salad.

Caramelized Pork

Servings: 6
Cooking Time: 17 Mins.

Ingredients:
- 2 lbs. pork shoulder, cut into 1½-inch thick slices
- 1/3 cup soy sauce
- 2 tbsps. sugar
- 1 tbsp. honey

Directions:
1. Preheat the Air fryer to 335 o F and grease an Air fryer basket.
2. Mix all the ingredients in a large bowl and coat chops well.
3. Cover and refrigerate for about 8 hours.
4. Arrange the chops in the Air fryer basket and cook for about 10 minutes, flipping once in between.
5. Set the Air fryer to 390 o F and cook for 7 more minutes.
6. Dish out in a platter and serve hot.

Sweet & Sour Pork Chops

Servings: 6
Cooking Time: 16 Mins.

Ingredients:
- 6 pork loin chops
- Salt and ground black pepper, as required
- 2 garlic cloves, minced
- 2 tbsps. honey
- 2 tbsps. soy sauce
- 1 tbsp. balsamic vinegar
- ¼ tsp. ground ginger

Directions:
1. With a meat tenderizer, tenderize the chops completely and then, sprinkle each with salt and black pepper.
2. In a large bowl, mix the remaining ingredients.
3. Add the chops and generously coat with marinade.
4. Cover and refrigerate for about 2-8 hours.
5. Set the temperature of air fryer to 355 degrees F. Grease an air fryer basket.
6. Arrange chops into the prepared air fryer basket in a single layer.
7. Air fry for about 6-8 minutes per side.
8. Remove from air fryer and transfer the chops onto plates.
9. Serve hot.

Cream Cheese Pork

Servings: 4
Cooking Time: 20 Mins.

Ingredients:
- 16 oz pork tenderloin
- 1 tsp. liquid smoke
- 1 tsp. mustard
- 1 tsp. cream cheese
- ½ tsp. ground paprika
- 1 tsp. avocado oil

Directions:
1. In the mixing bowl mix up liquid smoked, mustard, cream cheese, and ground paprika. Add avocado oil and. Stir the mixture. Then rub the pork tenderloin with the smoky mixture and wrap in the foil. Preheat the air fryer to 375F. Put the wrapped tenderloin in the air fryer basket and cook it for 20 minutes. Then discard the foil and slice the tenderloin into the servings.

Onion'n Garlic Rubbed Trip Tip

Servings: 4
Cooking Time: 50 Mins.

Ingredients:
- ½ cup red wine vinegar
- 1 tsp. garlic powder
- 1 tsp. onion powder
- 1-pound beef tri-tip
- 3 avocadoes, seeded and sliced
- 3 tbsps. olive oil

Directions:
1. In a Ziploc bag, place all ingredients except for the avocado slices.
2. Allow to marinate in the fridge for 2 hours.
3. Preheat the air fryer to 330oF.
4. Place the grill pan accessory in the air fryer.
5. Grill the avocado for 2 minutes while the beef is marinating. Set aside.
6. After two hours, grill the beef for 50 minutes. Flip the beef halfway through the cooking time.
7. Serve the beef with grilled avocadoes

Beef & Broccoli

Servings: 4
Cooking Time: 25 Mins.

Ingredients:
- 1 lb. broccoli, cut into florets
- ¾ lb. round steak, cut into strips
- 1 garlic clove, minced
- 1 tsp. ginger, minced
- 1 tbsp. olive oil
- 1 tsp. cornstarch
- 1 tsp. sugar
- 1 tsp. soy sauce
  - ⅓ cup sherry wine
- 2 tsp. sesame oil
  - ⅓ cup oyster sauce

Directions:
1. In a bowl, combine the sugar, soy sauce, sherry wine, cornstarch, sesame oil, and oyster sauce.
2. Place the steak strips in the bowl, coat each one with the mixture and allow to marinate for 45 minutes.
3. Put the broccoli in the Air Fryer and lay the steak on top.
4. Top with the olive oil, garlic and ginger.
5. Cook at 350°F for 12 minutes. Serve hot with rice if desired.

FISH & SEAFOOD RECIPES

Oregano Salmon

Servings: 2
Cooking Time: 7 Mins.

Ingredients:
- 10 oz salmon fillet
- 1 tsp. dried oregano
- 1 tsp. sesame oil
- 2 oz Parmesan, grated
- ¼ tsp. chili flakes

Directions:
1. Sprinkle the salmon fillet with dried oregano and chili flakes. Then brush it with sesame oil. Preheat the air fryer to 385F. Place the salmon in the air fryer basket and cook it for 5 minutes. Then flip the fish on another side and top with Parmesan. Cook the fish for 2 minutes more.

Cajun Shrimp

Servings: 4
Cooking Time: 25 Mins.

Ingredients:
- ¼ tsp. cayenne pepper
- ¼ tsp. smoked paprika
- ½ tsp. old bay seasoning
- 1 tbsp. olive oil
- Pinch of salt
- 1 ¼ lb. tiger shrimp

Directions:
1. Pre-heat your Air Fryer to 390°F.
2. In a large bowl, combine together all the ingredients, ensuring to coat the shrimps well.
3. Transfer to the fryer and cook for 5 minutes.
4. Serve over boiled rice.

Crumbly Fishcakes

Servings: 2
Cooking Time: 15 Mins.

Ingredients:
- 1 ½ oz potatoes, mashed
- A handful of capers
- A handful of parsley, chopped
- zest of 1 lemon
- 1 ¾ oz plain flour

Directions:
1. In a bowl, mix salmon, zest, capers, dill, and potatoes. Form small cakes and dust them with flour; refrigerate for 60 minutes. Preheat your air fryer to 350 and cook the cakes for 7 minutes. Serve chilled.

Butter Crab Muffins

Servings: 2
Cooking Time: 20 Mins.

Ingredients:
- 5 oz crab meat, chopped
- 2 eggs, beaten
- 2 tbsps. almond flour
- ¼ tsp. baking powder
- ½ tsp. apple cider vinegar
- ½ tsp. ground paprika
- 1 tbsp. butter, softened
- Cooking spray

Directions:
1. Grind the chopped crab meat and put it in the bowl. Add eggs, almond flour, baking powder, apple cider vinegar, ground paprika, and butter. Stir the mixture until homogenous. Preheat the air fryer to 365F. Spray the muffin molds with cooking spray. Then pour the crab meat batter in the muffin molds and place them in the preheated air fryer. Cook the crab muffins for 20 minutes or until they are light brown. Cool the cooked muffins to the room temperature and remove from the muffin mold.

Sesame Seeds Coated Haddock

Servings: 4
Cooking Time: 14 Mins.

Ingredients:
- 4 tbsps. plain flour
- 2 eggs
- ½ cup sesame seeds, toasted
- ½ cup breadcrumbs
- 4 (6-ounces) frozen haddock fillets
- 1/8 tsp. dried rosemary, crushed
- Salt and ground black pepper, as required
- 3 tbsps. olive oil

Directions:
1. Preheat the Air fryer to 390 o F and grease an Air fryer basket.
2. Place the flour in a shallow bowl and whisk the eggs in a second bowl.
3. Mix sesame seeds, breadcrumbs, rosemary, salt, black pepper and olive oil in a third bowl until a crumbly mixture is formed.
4. Coat each fillet with flour, dip into whisked eggs and finally, dredge into the breadcrumb mixture
5. Arrange haddock fillets into the Air fryer basket in a single layer and cook for about 14 minutes, flipping once in between.
6. Dish out the haddock fillets onto serving plates and serve hot.

Hot Tilapia

Servings: 2
Cooking Time: 9 Mins.

Ingredients:
- 1 chili pepper, chopped
- 1 tsp. chili flakes
- 1 tbsp. sesame oil
- ½ tsp. salt
- 10 oz tilapia fillet
- ¼ tsp. onion powder

Directions:
1. In the shallow bowl mix up chili pepper, chili flakes, salt, and onion powder. Gently churn the mixture and add sesame oil. After this, slice the tilapia fillet and sprinkle with chili mixture. Massage the fish with the help of the fingertips gently and leave for 10 minutes to marinate. Preheat the air fryer to 390F. Put the tilapia fillets in the air fryer basket and cook for 5 minutes. Then flip the fish on another side and cook for 4 minutes more.

Golden Cod Fish Nuggets

Servings: 4
Cooking Time: 20 Mins.

Ingredients:
- 2 tbsp olive oil
- 2 eggs, beaten
- 1 cup breadcrumbs
- A pinch of salt
- 1 cup flour

Directions:
1. Preheat air fryer to 390 F. Mix breadcrumbs, olive oil, and salt in a bowl until combined. in another bowl, place the eggs, and the flour into a third bowl. Toss the cod fillets in the flour, then in the eggs, and then in the breadcrumb mixture. Place in the fryer basket and cook for 9 minutes. At the 5-minute mark, quickly turn the chicken nuggets over. Once done, remove to a plate to serve.

Pesto Haddock

Servings: 2
Cooking Time: 8 Mins.

Ingredients:
- 2 (6-ounces) haddock fillets
- 1 tbsp. olive oil
- Salt and ground black pepper, as required
- 2 tbsps. pine nuts
- 3 tbsps. fresh basil, chopped
- 1 tbsp. Parmesan cheese, grated
- 1/3 cup extra-virgin olive oil

Directions:
1. Set the temperature of air fryer to 355 degrees F. Grease an air fryer basket.
2. Coat the fish fillets evenly with oil and then, sprinkle with salt and black pepper.
3. Arrange fish fillets into the prepared air fryer basket in a single layer.
4. Air fry for about 8 minutes.
5. Meanwhile, for the pesto: add the remaining ingredients in a food processor and pulse until smooth.
6. Remove from air fryer and transfer the flounder fillets onto serving plates.
7. Top with the pesto and serve.

Spanish Salmon Recipe

Servings: 6
Cooking Time: 25 Mins.

Ingredients:
- 2 cups bread croutons
- 3 red onions; cut into medium wedges
- 5 tbsp. olive oil
- 6 medium salmon fillets; skinless and boneless
- 2 tbsp. parsley; chopped
- 3/4 cup green olives; pitted
- 3 red bell peppers; cut into medium wedges
- 1/2 tsp. smoked paprika
- Salt and black pepper to the taste

Directions:
1. In a heat proof dish that fits your air fryer, mix bread croutons with onion wedges, bell pepper ones, olives, salt, pepper, paprika and 3 tbsp. olive oil; toss well, place in your air fryer and cook at 356 °F, for 7 minutes.
2. Rub salmon with the rest of the oil; add over veggies and cook at 360 °F, for 8 minutes. Divide fish and veggie mix on plates, sprinkle parsley all over and serve.

Sesame Tuna Steak

Servings: 2
Cooking Time: 12 Mins.

Ingredients:
- 1 tbsp. coconut oil, melted
- 2 x 6-oz. tuna steaks
- ½ tsp. garlic powder
- 2 tsp. black sesame seeds
- 2 tsp. white sesame seeds

Directions:
1. Apply the coconut oil to the tuna steaks with a brunch, then season with garlic powder.
2. Combine the black and white sesame seeds. Embed them in the tuna steaks, covering the fish all over. Place the tuna into your air fryer.
3. Cook for eight minutes at 400°F, turning the fish halfway through.
4. The tuna steaks are ready when they have reached a temperature of 145°F. Serve straightaway.

Fried Branzino

Servings: 4
Cooking Time: 20 Mins.

Ingredients:
- 4 medium branzino fillets; boneless
- 1/2 cup parsley; chopped
- 2 tbsp. olive oil
- A pinch of red pepper flakes; crushed
- Zest from 1 lemon; grated
- Zest from 1 orange; grated
- Juice from 1/2 lemon
- Juice from 1/2 orange
- Salt and black pepper to the taste

Directions:
1. In a large bowl; mix fish fillets with lemon zest, orange zest, lemon juice, orange juice, salt, pepper, oil and pepper flakes; toss really well, transfer fillets to your preheated air fryer at 350 °F and bake for 10 minutes; flipping fillets once. Divide fish on plates, sprinkle with parsley and serve right away.

POULTRY RECIPES

Crusted Chicken

Servings: 2
Cooking Time: 30 Mins.

Ingredients:
- ¼ cup slivered s
- 2x 6-oz. boneless skinless chicken breasts
- 2 tbsp. full-fat mayonnaise
- 1 tbsp. Dijon mustard

Directions:
1. Pulse the s in a food processor until they are finely chopped. Spread the s on a plate and set aside.
2. Cut each chicken breast in half lengthwise.
3. Mix the mayonnaise and mustard together and then spread evenly on top of the chicken slices.
4. Place the chicken into the plate of chopped s to coat completely, laying each coated slice into the basket of your fryer.
5. Cook for 25 minutes at 350°F until golden. Test the temperature, making sure the chicken has reached 165°F. Serve hot.

Five Spice Duck Legs

Servings: 4
Cooking Time: 25 Mins.

Ingredients:
- 4 duck legs
- 2 garlic cloves, minced
- 1 tsp. five spice
- A pinch of salt and black pepper
- 2 tbsps. olive oil
- 1 tsp. hot chili powder

Directions:
1. In a bowl, mix the duck legs with all the other ingredients and rub them well. Put the duck legs in your air fryer's basket and cook at 380 degrees F for 25 minutes, flipping them halfway. Divide between plates and serve.

Texas Bbq Chicken Thighs

Servings: 4
Cooking Time: 30 Mins.

Ingredients:
- Salt and black pepper to taste
- 2 tsp Texas BBQ Jerky seasoning
- 1 tbsp olive oil
- 2 tbsp cilantro, chopped

Directions:
1. Preheat the Air fryer to 380 F. Grease the air fryer basket with cooking spray.
2. Drizzle the chicken with olive oil, season with salt and pepper, and sprinkle over BBQ seasoning. Place in the air fryer basket. Cook for 20 minutes. Serve sprinkled with cilantro.

Duck Breasts and Raspberry Sauce Recipe

Servings: 4
Cooking Time: 25 Mins.

Ingredients:
- 2 duck breasts; skin on and scored
- 1 tbsp. sugar
- 1 tsp. red wine vinegar
- 1/2 cup raspberries
- 1/2 cup water
- 1/2 tsp. cinnamon powder
- Salt and black pepper to the taste
- Cooking spray

Directions:
1. Season duck breasts with salt and pepper, spray them with cooking spray, put in preheated air fryer skin side down and cook at 350 °F, for 10 minutes.
2. Heat up a pan with the water over medium heat, add raspberries, cinnamon, sugar and wine; stir, bring to a simmer, transfer to your blender, puree and return to pan. Add air fryer duck breasts to pan as well; toss to coat, divide among plates and serve right away.

Authentic Mexican Mole

Servings: 4
Cooking Time: 35 Mins.

Ingredients:
- 8 chicken thighs, skinless, bone-in
- 1 tbsp. peanut oil
- Sea salt and ground black pepper, to taste
- Mole sauce:
- 1 tbsp. peanut oil
- 1 onion, chopped
- 1 oz. dried negro chiles, stemmed, seeded, and chopped
- 2 garlic cloves, peeled and halved
- 1 large-sized fresh tomatoes, pureed
- 1 ½ ozs. sugar-free bakers' chocolate, chopped
- 1 tsp. dried Mexican oregano
- 1/2 tsp. ground cumin
- 1 tsp. coriander seeds
- A pinch of ground cloves
- 1/4 cup almonds, slivered and toasted

Directions:
1. Start by preheating your Air Fryer to 380 degrees F. Toss the chicken thighs with the peanut oil, salt, and black pepper.
2. Cook in the preheated Air Fryer for 12 minutes; flip them and cook an additional 10 minutes; reserve.
3. To make the sauce, heat 1 tbsp. of peanut oil in a saucepan over medium-high heat. Now, sauté the onion, chiles and garlic until fragrant or about 2 minutes.
4. Next, stir in the tomatoes, chocolate, oregano, cumin, coriander seeds, and cloves. Let it simmer until the sauce has slightly thickened.
5. Add the reserved chicken to the baking pan; add the sauce and cook in the preheated Air Fryer at 360 degrees F for 10 minutes or until thoroughly warmed.
6. Serve garnished with slivered almonds. Enjoy!

Lemon and Chili Chicken Drumsticks

Servings: 6
Cooking Time: 20 Mins.

Ingredients:
- 6 chicken drumsticks
- 1 tsp. dried oregano
- 1 tbsp. lemon juice
- ½ tsp. lemon zest, grated
- 1 tsp. ground cumin
- ½ tsp. chili flakes
- 1 tsp. garlic powder
- ½ tsp. ground coriander
- 1 tbsp. avocado oil

Directions:
1. Rub the chicken drumsticks with dried oregano, lemon juice, lemon zest, ground cumin, chili flakes, garlic powder, and ground coriander. Then sprinkle them with avocado oil and put in the air fryer. Cook the chicken drumsticks for 20 minutes at 375F.

Bacon-wrapped Chicken

Servings: 6
Cooking Time: 20 Mins.

Ingredients:
- 1 chicken breast, cut into 6 pieces
- 6 rashers back bacon
- 1 tbsp. soft cheese

Directions:
1. Put the bacon rashers on a flat surface and cover one side with the soft cheese.
2. Lay the chicken pieces on each bacon rasher. Wrap the bacon around the chicken and use a toothpick stick to hold each one in place. Put them in Air Fryer basket.
3. Air fry at 350°F for 15 minutes.

Turkey & Veggie Skewers

Servings: 4
Cooking Time: 20 Mins.

Ingredients:
- 1 lb. turkey breast, cubed
- 2 tbsp chopped fresh rosemary
- Salt and black pepper to taste
- 1 green bell pepper, cut into chunks
- 1 red bell pepper, cut into chunks
- 1 cup cherry tomatoes
- 1 red onion, cut into wedges

Directions:
1. Preheat your Air Fryer to 350 F. Spray the air fryer basket with cooking spray.
2. In a bowl, mix the turkey, salt, and black pepper. Thread the vegetables and turkey cubes alternately onto the skewers. Spray with cooking spray and transfer to the cooking basket. Cook for 15 minutes, flipping once halfway through. Serve sprinkled with rosemary.

Garden Vegetable and Chicken Casserole

Servings: 4
Cooking Time: 30 Mins.

Ingredients:
- 2 tsps. peanut oil
- 2 lbs. chicken drumettes
- 1 garlic clove, minced
- 1/2 medium-sized leek, sliced
- 2 carrots, sliced
- 1 cup cauliflower florets
- 1 tbsp. all-purpose flour
- 2 cups vegetable broth
- 1/4 cup dry white wine
- 1 thyme sprig
- 1 rosemary sprig

Directions:
1. Preheat your Air Fryer to 370 degrees F. Then, drizzle the chicken drumettes with peanut oil and cook them for 10 minutes. Transfer the chicken drumettes to a lightly greased pan.
2. Add the garlic, leeks, carrots, and cauliflower.
3. Mix the remaining ingredients in a bowl. Pour the flour mixture into the pan. Cook at 380 degrees F for 15 minutes.
4. Serve warm.

Naked Cheese, Chicken Stuffing 'n Green Beans

Servings: 3
Cooking Time: 20 Mins.

Ingredients:
- 1 cup cooked, cubed chicken breast meat
- 1/2 (10.75 ounce) can condensed cream of chicken soup
- 1/2 (14.5 ounce) can green beans, drained
- 1/2 cup shredded Cheddar cheese
- 6-ounce unseasoned dry bread stuffing mix
- salt and pepper to taste

Directions:
1. Mix well pepper, salt, soup, and chicken in a medium bowl.
2. Make the stuffing according to package Directions for Cooking.
3. Lightly grease baking pan of air fryer with cooking spray. Evenly spread chicken mixture on bottom of pan. Top evenly with stuffing. Sprinkle cheese on top.
4. Cover pan with foil.
5. For 15 minutes, cook on 390oF.
6. Remove foil and cook for 5 minutes at 390oF until tops are lightly browned.
7. Serve and enjoy.

Middle Eastern Chicken Bbq with Tzatziki Sauce

Servings: 6
Cooking Time: 24 Mins.

Ingredients:

- 1 1/2 lbs. skinless, boneless chicken breast halves - cut into bite-sized pieces
- 1 tsp. dried oregano
- 1/2 tsp. salt
- 1/4 cup olive oil
- 2 cloves garlic, minced
- 2 tbsps. lemon juice
- Tzatziki Dip Ingredients
- 1 (6 ounce) container plain Greek-style yogurt
- 1 tbsp. olive oil
- 2 tsps. white vinegar
- 1 clove garlic, minced
- 1 pinch salt
- 1/2 cucumber - peeled, seeded, and grated

Directions:

1. In a medium bowl mix well, all Tzatziki dip Ingredients. Refrigerate for at least 2 hours to allow flavors to blend.
2. In a resealable bag, mix well salt, oregano, garlic, lemon juice, and olive oil. Add chicken, squeeze excess air, seal, and marinate for at least 2 hours.
3. Thread chicken into skewers and place on skewer rack. Cook in batches.
4. For 12 minutes, cook on 360oF. Halfway through cooking time, turnover skewers and baste with marinade from resealable bag.
5. Serve and enjoy with Tzatziki dip.

VEGETABLE & SIDE DISHES

Greek-style Roasted Vegetable Salad

Servings: 4
Cooking Time: 20 Mins.

Ingredients:
- 1 red onion, sliced
- 1 lb. cherry tomatoes
- 1/2 lb. asparagus
- 1 cucumber, sliced
- 2 cups baby spinach
- 2 tbsps. white vinegar
- 1/4 cup extra-virgin olive oil
- 2 tbsps. fresh parsley
- Sea salt and pepper to taste
- 1/2 cup Kalamata olives, pitted and sliced

Directions:
1. Begin by preheating your Air Fryer to 400 degrees F.
2. Place the onion, cherry tomatoes, and asparagus in the lightly greased Air Fryer basket. Bake for 5 to 6 minutes, tossing the basket occasionally.
3. Transfer to a salad bowl. Add the cucumber and baby spinach.
4. Then, whisk the vinegar, olive oil, parsley, salt, and black pepper in a small mixing bowl. Dress your salad; add Kalamata olives.
5. Toss to combine well and serve.

Asparagus and Green Beans Salad

Servings: 3
Cooking Time: 6 Mins.

Ingredients:
- 3 oz asparagus, chopped
- 2 oz green beans, chopped
- 1 cup arugula, chopped
- 1 tbsp. hazelnuts, chopped
- 1 tsp. flax seeds
- 2 oz Mozzarella, chopped
- 1 tbsp. olive oil
- ½ tsp. salt
- ½ tsp. ground paprika
- ½ tsp. ground black pepper
- Cooking spray

Directions:
1. Preheat the air fryer to 400F. Put the asparagus and green beans in the air fryer and spray them with cooking spray. Cook the vegetables for 6 minutes at 400F. Shake the vegetables after 3 minutes of cooking. Then cool them to the room temperature and put in the salad bowl. Add hazelnuts, flax seeds, chopped Mozzarella, salt, ground paprika, and ground black pepper. Sprinkle the salad with olive oil and shake well.

Roasted Brussels Sprout Salad

Servings: 2
Cooking Time: 35 Minutes + Chilling Time

Ingredients:
- 1/2 lb. Brussels sprouts
- 1 tbsp. olive oil
- Coarse sea salt and ground black pepper, to taste
- 2 ozs. baby arugula
- 1 shallot, thinly sliced
- 2 ozs. pancetta, chopped
- Lemon Vinaigrette:
- 2 tbsps. extra virgin olive oil
- 2 tbsps. fresh lemon juice
- 1 tbsp. honey
- 1 tsp. Dijon mustard

Directions:
1. Start by preheating your Air Fryer to 380 degrees F.
2. Add the Brussels sprouts to the cooking basket. Brush with olive oil and cook for 15 minutes. Let it cool to room temperature about 15 minutes.
3. Toss the Brussels sprouts with the salt, black pepper, baby arugula, and shallot.
4. Mix all ingredients for the dressing. Then, dress your salad, garnish with pancetta, and serve well chilled. Bon appétit!

Parmesan Cauliflower Risotto

Servings: 4
Cooking Time: 18 Mins.

Ingredients:
- 1 cup cauliflower, shredded
- 4 oz cremini mushrooms, sliced
- 2 oz Parmesan, grated
- 1 tsp. ground black pepper
- 1 tbsp. heavy cream
- ¼ tsp. garlic powder
- 3 spring onions, diced
- 1 tbsp. olive oil
- ½ tsp. Italian seasonings

Directions:
1. Preheat the air fryer to 400f. Then sprinkle the air fryer basket with olive oil. Place the mushrooms inside and sprinkle them with ground black pepper. Cook them at 400F for 4 minutes. Then stir them well and add the spring onion. Cook the vegetables for 4 minutes more. Then shake them well and sprinkle with garlic powder and Italian seasonings. Mix up well and transfer in the air fryer mold. Add heavy cream and shredded cauliflower. Then add parmesan and mix up. Place the mold in the air fryer and cook for 10 minutes at 375F. Then mix up risotto and transfer in the serving plates.

Gluten-free Beans

Servings: 2
Cooking Time: 10 Mins.

Ingredients:
- 8 oz green beans, cut ends and cut beans in half
- 1 tsp sesame oil
- 1 tbsp tamari

Directions:
1. Add all ingredients into the zip-lock bag and shake well.
2. Place green beans into the air fryer basket and cook at 400 F for 10 minutes. Turn halfway through.
3. Serve and enjoy.

Coconut Celery and Broccoli Mash

Servings: 2
Cooking Time: 5 Mins.

Ingredients:
- 7 oz broccoli florets
- 1 tbsp. almond butter
- ½ tsp. salt
- 2 oz celery stalk, chopped
- 2 tbsps. coconut cream
- Cooking spray

Directions:
1. Preheat the air fryer to 400F. Then put the broccoli florets and celery stalk in the air fryer basket and spray them with cooking spray. Cook the vegetables for 5 minutes at 400F. Then put the cooked vegetables in the blender and blend them until you get a puree. After this, put the puree in the bowl. Add salt, almond butter, and coconut cream. Stir the puree with the help of the spoon.

Sweet Corn Fritters

Servings: 4
Cooking Time: 20 Mins.

Ingredients:
- 1 medium-sized carrot, grated
- 1 yellow onion, finely chopped
- 4 oz. canned sweet corn kernels, drained
- 1 tsp. sea salt flakes
- 1 heaping tbsp. fresh cilantro, chopped
- 1 medium-sized egg, whisked
- 2 tbsp. plain milk
- 1 cup of Parmesan cheese, grated
- ¼ cup flour
  - ⅓ tsp. baking powder
  - ⅓ tsp. sugar

Directions:
1. Place the grated carrot in a colander and press down to squeeze out any excess moisture. Dry it with a paper towel.
2. Combine the carrots with the remaining ingredients.
3. Mold 1 tbsp. of the mixture into a ball and press it down with your hand or a spoon to flatten it. Repeat until the rest of the mixture is used up.
4. Spritz the balls with cooking spray.
5. Arrange in the basket of your Air Fryer, taking care not to overlap any balls. Cook at 350°F for 8 to 11 minutes or until they're firm.
6. Serve warm.

Fried Yellow Beans with Blue Cheese and Pecans

Servings: 3
Cooking Time: 15 Mins.

Ingredients:
- 3/4 lb. wax yellow beans, cleaned
- 2 tbsps. peanut oil
- 4 tbsps. Romano cheese, grated
- Sea salt and ground black pepper, to taste
- 1/2 tsp. red pepper flakes, crushed
- 2 tbsps. pecans, sliced
- 1/3 cup blue cheese, crumbled

Directions:
1. Toss the wax beans with the peanut oil, Romano cheese, salt, black pepper, and red pepper.
2. Place the wax beans in the lightly greased cooking basket.
3. Cook in the preheated Air Fryer at 400 degrees F for 5 minutes. Shake the basket once or twice.
4. Add the pecans and cook for 3 minutes more or until lightly toasted. Serve topped with blue cheese and enjoy!

Mushroom Cakes

Servings: 4
Cooking Time: 8 Mins.

Ingredients:
- 9 oz mushrooms, finely chopped
- ¼ cup coconut flour
- 1 tsp. salt
- 1 egg, beaten
- 3 oz Cheddar cheese, shredded
- 1 tsp. dried parsley
- ½ tsp. ground black pepper
- 1 tsp. sesame oil
- 1 oz spring onion, chopped

Directions:
1. In the mixing bowl mix up chopped mushrooms, coconut flour, salt, egg, dried parsley, ground black pepper, and minced onion. Stir the mixture until smooth and add Cheddar cheese. Stir it with the help of the fork, Preheat the air fryer to 385F. Line the air fryer pan with baking paper. with the help of the spoon make the medium size patties and put them in the pan. Sprinkle the patties with sesame oil and cook for 4 minutes from each side.

Japanese Tempura Bowl

Servings: 3
Cooking Time: 20 Mins.

Ingredients:
- 1 cup all-purpose flour
- Kosher salt and ground black pepper, to taste
- 1/2 tsp. paprika
- 2 eggs
- 3 tbsps. soda water
- 1 cup panko crumbs
- 2 tbsps. olive oil
- 1 cup green beans
- 1 onion, cut into rings
- 1 zucchini, cut into slices
- 2 tbsps. soy sauce
- 1 tbsp. mirin
- 1 tsp. dashi granules

Directions:
1. In a shallow bowl, mix the flour, salt, black pepper, and paprika. in a separate bowl, whisk the eggs and soda water. in a third shallow bowl, combine the panko crumbs with olive oil.
2. Dip the vegetables in flour mixture, then in the egg mixture; lastly, roll over the panko mixture to coat evenly.
3. Cook in the preheated Air Fryer at 400 degrees F for 10 minutes, shaking the basket halfway through the cooking time. Work in batches until the vegetables are crispy and golden brown.
4. Then, make the sauce by whisking the soy sauce, mirin, and dashi granules. Bon appétit!

Hot Broccoli

Servings: 4
Cooking Time: 5 Mins.

Ingredients:
- 11 oz broccoli stems
- 1 tbsp. olive oil
- ¼ tsp. chili powder

Directions:
1. Preheat the air fryer to 400F. Then chop the broccoli stems roughly and sprinkle with chili powder and olive oil. Transfer the greens in the preheated air fryer and cook them for 5 minutes.

SNACKS & APPETIZERS RECIPES

Feta Triangles

Servings: 5
Cooking Time: 55 Mins.

Ingredients:
- 1 egg yolk, beaten
- 4 oz. feta cheese
- 2 tbsp. flat-leafed parsley, finely chopped
- 1 scallion, finely chopped
- 2 sheets of frozen filo pastry, defrosted
- 2 tbsp. olive oil ground black pepper to taste

Directions:
1. 1 in a bowl, combine the beaten egg yolk with the feta, parsley and scallion. Sprinkle on some pepper to taste.
2. 2 Slice each sheet of filo dough into three strips.
3. 3 Place a teaspoonful of the feta mixture on each strip of pastry.
4. 4 Pinch the tip of the pastry and fold it up to enclose the filling and create a triangle. Continue folding the strip in zig-zags until the filling is wrapped in a triangle. Repeat with all of the strips of pastry.
5. 5 Pre-heat the Air Fryer to 390°F.
6. 6 Coat the pastry with a light coating of oil and arrange in the cooking basket.
7. 7 Place the basket in the Air Fryer and cook for 3 minutes.
8. 8 Lower the heat to 360°F and cook for a further 2 minutes or until a golden brown color is achieved

Party Chicken Pillows

Servings: 4
Cooking Time: 20 Mins.

Ingredients:
- 1 tsp. olive oil
- 1 cup ground chicken
- 1 (8-ounces) can Pillsbury Crescent Roll dough
- Sea salt and ground black pepper, to taste
- 1 tsp. onion powder
- 1/2 tsp. garlic powder
- 4 tbsps. tomato paste
- 4 ozs. cream cheese, at room temperature
- 2 tbsps. butter, melted

Directions:
1. Heat the olive oil in a pan over medium-high heat. Then, cook the ground chicken until browned or about 4 minutes.
2. Unroll the crescent dough. Roll out the dough using a rolling pin; cut into 8 pieces.
3. Place the browned chicken, salt, black pepper, onion powder, garlic powder, tomato paste, and cheese in the center of each piece.
4. Fold each corner over the filling using wet hands. Press together to cover the filling entirely and seal the edges.
5. Now, spritz the bottom of the Air Fryer basket with cooking oil. Lay the chicken pillows in a single layer in the cooking basket. Drizzle the melted butter all over chicken pillows.
6. Bake at 370 degrees F for 6 minutes or until golden brown. Work in batches. Bon appétit!

Cheese Filled Bell Peppers

Servings: 3
Cooking Time: 12 Mins.

Ingredients:
- 1 small green bell pepper
- 1 small red bell pepper
- 1 small yellow bell pepper
- ½ cup mozzarella cheese
- ½ cup cream cheese
- 3 tsps. red chili flakes

Directions:
1. Preheat the Air fryer to 320 o F and grease an Air fryer basket.
2. Chop the tops of the bell peppers and remove all the seeds.
3. Mix together mozzarella cheese, cream cheese and red chili flakes in a bowl.
4. Stuff this cheese mixture in the bell peppers and put back the tops.
5. Arrange in the Air Fryer basket and cook for about 12 minutes.
6. Remove from the Air fryer and serve hot.

Snack Mix

Servings: 10
Cooking Time: 30 Mins.

Ingredients:
- ½ cup honey
- 3 tbsp. butter, melted
- 1 tsp. salt
- 2 cups sesame sticks
- 2 cup pepitas [pumpkin seeds]
- 2 cups granola
- 1 cup cashews
- 2 cups crispy corn puff cereal [Kix or Corn Pops]
- 2 cup mini pretzel crisps

Directions:
1. 1 in a bowl, combine the honey, butter, and salt.
2. 2 in another bowl, mix together the sesame sticks, pepitas, granola, cashews, corn puff cereal, and pretzel crisps.
3. 3 Combine the contents of the two bowls.
4. 4 Pre-heat your Air Fryer to 370°F.
5. 5 Put the mixture in the fryer basket and air-fry for 10 - 12 minutes to toast the snack mixture, shaking the basket frequently. You will have to do this in two batches.
6. 6 Place the snack mix on a cookie sheet and allow it to cool fully.
7. 7 Store in an airtight container for up to one week. Makes a great holiday gift!

Bbq Lil Smokies

Servings: 6
Cooking Time: 20 Mins.

Ingredients:
- 1 lb. beef cocktail wieners
- 10 ozs. barbecue sauce, no sugar added

Directions:
1. Start by preheating your Air Fryer to 380 degrees F.
2. Prick holes into your sausages using a fork and transfer them to the baking pan.
3. Cook for 13 minutes. Spoon the barbecue sauce into the pan and cook an additional 2 minutes.
4. Serve with toothpicks. Bon appétit!

Broccoli Fries with Spicy Dip

Servings: 4
Cooking Time: 15 Mins.

Ingredients:
- 3/4 lb. broccoli florets
- 1/2 tsp. onion powder
- 1 tsp. granulated garlic
- 1/2 tsp. cayenne pepper
- Sea salt and ground black pepper, to taste
- 2 tbsps. sesame oil
- 4 tbsps. parmesan cheese, preferably freshly grated
- Spicy Dip:
- 1/4 cup mayonnaise
- 1/4 cup Greek yogurt
- 1/4 tsp. Dijon mustard
- 1 tsp. hot sauce

Directions:
1. Start by preheating the Air Fryer to 400 degrees F.
2. Blanch the broccoli in salted boiling water until al dente, about 3 to 4 minutes. Drain well and transfer to the lightly greased Air Fryer basket.
3. Add the onion powder, garlic, cayenne pepper, salt, black pepper, sesame oil, and parmesan cheese.
4. Cook for 6 minutes, tossing halfway through the cooking time.
5. Meanwhile, mix all of the spicy dip ingredients. Serve broccoli fries with chilled dipping sauce. Bon appétit!

Bacon Dip

Servings: 12
Cooking Time: 20 Mins.

Ingredients:
- 2 tbsps. ghee, melted
- 3 cups spring onions, chopped
- A pinch of salt and black pepper
- 2 ozs. cheddar cheese, shredded
- 1/3 cup coconut cream
- 6 bacon slices, cooked and crumbled

Directions:
1. Heat up a pan that fits the fryer with the ghee over medium-high heat, add the onions, stir and sauté for 7 minutes. Add the remaining ingredients, except the bacon and stir well. Sprinkle the bacon on top, introduce the pan in the machine and cook at and 380 degrees F for 13 minutes. Divide into bowls and serve as a party dip.

Cheesy Potatoes

Servings: 4
Cooking Time: 20 Mins.

Ingredients:
- 11 oz. potatoes, diced and boiled
- 1 egg yolk
- 2 tbsp. flour
- 3 tbsp. parmesan cheese
- 3 tbsp. friendly bread crumbs, tossed with a little oil
- Pepper to taste
- Nutmeg to taste
- Salt to taste

Directions:
1. Pre-heat Air Fryer at 390°F.
2. Mash up the potatoes and combine with all of the ingredients, minus the bread crumbs.
3. Shape equal amounts of the mixture into medium-sized balls and roll each one in the bread crumbs.
4. Place the potato balls in the fryer and cook for 4 minutes.

Broccoli Florets

Servings: 4
Cooking Time: 20 Mins.

Ingredients:
- 1 lb. broccoli, cut into florets
- 1 tbsp. lemon juice
- 1 tbsp. olive oil
- 1 tbsp. sesame seeds
- 3 garlic cloves, minced

Directions:
1. In a bowl, combine all of the ingredients, coating the broccoli well.
2. Transfer to the Air Fryer basket and air fry at 400°F for 13 minutes.

Barbecue Little Smokies

Servings: 6
Cooking Time: 20 Mins.

Ingredients:
- 1 lb. beef cocktail wieners
- 10 ozs. barbecue sauce

Directions:
1. Start by preheating your Air Fryer to 380 degrees F.
2. Prick holes into your sausages using a fork and transfer them to the baking pan.
3. Cook for 13 minutes. Spoon the barbecue sauce into the pan and cook an additional 2 minutes.
4. Serve with toothpicks. Bon appétit!

Masala Cashew

Servings: 3
Cooking Time: 20 Mins.

Ingredients:
- ½ lb. cashew nuts
- ½ tsp. garam masala powder
- 1 tsp. coriander powder
- 1 tsp. ghee
- 1 tsp. red chili powder
- ½ tsp. black pepper
- 2 tsp. dry mango powder
- 1 tsp. sea salt

Directions:
1. 1 Put all the ingredients in a large bowl and toss together well.
2. 2 Arrange the cashew nuts in the basket of your Air Fryer.
3. 3 Cook at 250°F for 15 minutes until the nuts are brown and crispy.
4. 4 Let the nuts cool before serving or transferring to an airtight container to be stored for up to 2 weeks.

VEGAN & VEGETARIAN RECIPES

Root Vegetable Medley

Servings: 4
Cooking Time: 30 Mins.

Ingredients:
- 2 carrots, sliced
- 1 turnip, peeled and cut into chunks
- 1 rutabaga, peeled and cut into chunks
- 2 potatoes, peeled and cut into chunks
- 1 beet, peeled and cut into chunks
- Salt and black pepper to taste
- 2 tbsp fresh thyme, chopped
- 2 tbsp olive oil
- 2 tbsp tomato pesto

Directions:
1. Preheat the Air fryer to 400 F.
2. In a bowl, combine all the root vegetables, salt, pepper, and olive oil. Toss to coat and transfer to air fryer basket. Cook for 12 minutes, then shake and continue cooking for another 10 minutes. Combine the pesto with 2 tbsp water and drizzle over the vegetables, then sprinkle with thyme to serve.

Crispy Asparagus Dipped in Paprika-garlic Spice

Servings: 5
Cooking Time: 15 Mins.

Ingredients:
- ¼ cup almond flour
- ½ tsp. garlic powder
- ½ tsp. smoked paprika
- 10 medium asparagus, trimmed
- 2 large eggs, beaten
- 2 tbsps. parsley, chopped
- Salt and pepper to taste

Directions:
1. Preheat the air fryer for 5 minutes.
2. In a mixing bowl, combine the parsley, garlic powder, almond flour, and smoked paprika. Season with salt and pepper to taste.
3. Soak firs the asparagus in the beaten eggs and dredge in the almond flour mixture.
4. Place in the air fryer basket. Close.
5. Cook for 15 minutes at 350oF.

Roasted Mushrooms in Herb-garlic Oil

Servings: 4
Cooking Time: 25 Mins.

Ingredients:
- ½ tsp. minced garlic
- 2 lbs. mushrooms
- 2 tsps. herbs de Provence
- 3 tbsps. coconut oil
- Salt and pepper to taste

Directions:
1. Preheat the air fryer for 5 minutes.
2. Place all ingredients in a baking dish that will fit in the air fryer.
3. Mix to combine.
4. Place the baking dish in the air fryer.
5. Cook for 25 minutes at 350oF.

Aromatic Baked Potatoes with Chives

Servings: 2
Cooking Time: 45 Mins.

Ingredients:
- 4 medium baking potatoes, peeled
- 2 tbsps. olive oil
- 1/4 tsp. red pepper flakes
- 1/4 tsp. smoked paprika
- 1 tbsp. sea salt
- 2 garlic cloves, minced
- 2 tbsps. chives, chopped

Directions:
1. Toss the potatoes with the olive oil, seasoning, and garlic.
2. Place them in the Air Fryer basket. Cook in the preheated Air Fryer at 400 degrees F for 40 minutes or until fork tender.
3. Garnish with fresh chopped chives. Bon appétit!

Thai Sweet Potato Balls

Servings: 4
Cooking Time: 50 Mins.

Ingredients:
- 1 lb. sweet potatoes
- 1 cup brown sugar
- 1 tbsp. orange juice
- 2 tsps. orange zest
- 1/2 tsp. ground cinnamon
- 1/4 tsp. ground cloves
- 1/2 cup almond meal
- 1 tsp. baking powder
- 1 cup coconut flakes

Directions:
1. Bake the sweet potatoes at 380 degrees F for 30 to 35 minutes until tender; peel and mash them.
2. Add the brown sugar, orange juice, orange zest, ground cinnamon, cloves, almond meal, and baking powder; mix to combine well.
3. Roll the balls in the coconut flakes.
4. Bake in the preheated Air Fryer at 360 degrees F for 15 minutes or until thoroughly cooked and crispy.
5. Repeat the process until you run out of ingredients. Bon appétit!

Broccoli with Olives

Servings: 4
Cooking Time: 19 Mins.

Ingredients:
- 2 lbs. broccoli, stemmed and cut into 1-inch florets
- 1/3 cup Kalamata olives, halved and pitted
- ¼ cup Parmesan cheese, grated
- 2 tbsps. olive oil
- Salt and ground black pepper, as required
- 2 tsps. fresh lemon zest, grated

Directions:
1. Preheat the Air fryer to 400 o F and grease an Air fryer basket.
2. Boil the broccoli for about 4 minutes and drain well.
3. Mix broccoli, oil, salt, and black pepper in a bowl and toss to coat well.
4. Arrange broccoli into the Air fryer basket and cook for about 15 minutes.
5. Stir in the olives, lemon zest and cheese and dish out to serve.

Cheddar, Squash 'n Zucchini Casserole

Servings: 4
Cooking Time: 30 Mins.

Ingredients:

- 1 egg
- 5 saltine crackers, or as needed, crushed
- 2 tbsps. bread crumbs
- 1/2-pound yellow squash, sliced
- 1/2-pound zucchini, sliced
- 1/2 cup shredded Cheddar cheese
- 1-1/2 tsps. white sugar
- 1/2 tsp. salt
- 1/4 onion, diced
- 1/4 cup biscuit baking mix
- 1/4 cup butter

Directions:

1. Lightly grease baking pan of air fryer with cooking spray. Add onion, zucchini, and yellow squash. Cover pan with foil and for 15 minutes, cook on 360oF or until tender.
2. Stir in salt, sugar, egg, butter, baking mix, and cheddar cheese. Mix well. Fold in crushed crackers. Top with bread crumbs.
3. Cook for 15 minutes at 390oF until tops are lightly browned.
4. Serve and enjoy.

Spiced Up Potato Wedges

Servings: 6
Cooking Time: 30 Mins.

Ingredients:
- 2 tbsp olive oil
- 2 tsp smoked paprika
- 2 tbsp sriracha hot chili sauce
- ½ cup Greek yogurt

Directions:
1. Soak potatoes under cold water for 30 minutes; pat dry with a towel. Preheat your air fryer to 340 F, and coat potatoes with oil and paprika. Cook them for 20 minutes, shaking once halfway through.Remove to a paper to let them dry; season with salt and pepper. Serve with the yogurt and chili sauce .

Grilled 'n Glazed Strawberries

Servings: 2
Cooking Time: 20 Mins.

Ingredients:
- 1 tbsp honey
- 1 tsp lemon zest
- 1-lb large strawberries
- 3 tbsp melted butter
- Lemon wedges
- Pinch kosher salt

Directions:
1. Thread strawberries in 4 skewers.
2. In a small bowl, mix well remaining Ingredients except for lemon wedges. Brush all over strawberries.
3. Place skewer on air fryer skewer rack.
4. For 10 minutes, cook on 360oF. Halfway through cooking time, brush with honey mixture and turnover skewer.
5. Serve and enjoy with a squeeze of lemon.

Teriyaki Cauliflower4

Servings: 4
Cooking Time: 20 Mins.

Ingredients:
- ½ cup soy sauce
- 3 tbsp brown sugar
- 1 tsp sesame oil
- ⅓ cup water
- ½ chili powder
- 2 cloves garlic, chopped
- 1 tsp cornstarch

Directions:
1. In a bowl, whisk soy sauce, sugar, sesame oil, water, chili powder, garlic and cornstarch, until smooth. in a bowl, add cauliflower, and pour teriyaki sauce over the top, toss with hands until well-coated.
2. Take the cauliflower to the air fryer's basket and cook for 14 minutes at 340 F, turning once halfway through. When ready, check if the cauliflower is cooked but not too soft. Serve with rice.

Paneer Cutlet

Servings: 1
Cooking Time: 15 Mins.

Ingredients:
- 1 cup grated cheese
- ½ tsp chai masala
- 1 tsp butter
- ½ tsp garlic powder
- 1 small onion, finely chopped
- ½ tsp oregano
- ½ tsp salt

Directions:
1. Preheat the air fryer to 350 F, and grease a baking dish. Mix all ingredients in a bowl, until well incorporated. Make cutlets out of the mixture and place them on the greased baking dish. Place the baking dish in the air fryer and cook the cutlets for 10 minutes, until crispy.

Printed in Great Britain
by Amazon

79879506R00066